The Bill of Rights

KAREN PRICE HOSSELL

Heinemann Library
Chicago, Illinois

Designed by Herman Adler Design
Photo research by Bill Broyles
Printed and bound in the United States by Lake Book
Manufacturing, Inc.

08 07 06 05 04
10 9 8 7 6 5 4 3 2 1

Library of Congress Cataloging-in-Publication Data
Price Hossell, Karen, 1957-
  The Bill of Rights / Karen Price Hossell.
    p. cm. -- (Historical documents)
Summary: Provides a history of the Bill of Rights, explains
each of the amendments and the freedoms it protects, and
describes how historical documents such as this can be
restored and preserved.
Includes bibliographical references and index.
  ISBN 1-4034-0801-7 (hardcover) -- ISBN 1-4034-3430-1
(pbk.)
  1. United States. Constitution. 1st-10th Amendments--
Juvenile literature. [1. United States. Constitution. 1st-10th
Amendments. 2. Constitutional amendments. 3. Civil rights.]
I. Title. II. Historical documents (Heinemann Library (Firm))
  KF4750.P75 2003
  342.73'03--dc21
                              2003008192

Acknowledgments
The author and publisher are grateful to the following
for permission to reproduce copyright material:

Cover photographs by (document) National Archives and
Records Administration, (portraits, T-B) Bettmann/Corbis,
Gift of the Regents of the Smithsonian Institution/The
Thomas Jefferson Memorial Foundation and the Enid
and Crosby Kemper Foundation/Owned jointly with
Monticello/National Portrait Gallery, Smithsonian
Institution/Art Resource, NY, Réunion des Musées
Nationaux/Art Resource, NY (title bar) Corbis.

Title page (L-R) Rick Bowmer/AP Wide World Photos,
National Archives and Records Administration; pp. 4, 8,
24, 29t, 32, 35, 38, 40, 41, 42 National Archives and
Records Administration; pp. 5, 9, 10, 17, 18, 25, 28
Bettmann/Corbis; pp. 6, 14, 26, 36 Library of Congress;
p. 15 The Granger Collection, New York;
pp. 7, 43, 44 Alex Wong/Getty Images; p. 11 Réunion des
Musées Nationaux/Art Resource, NY; p. 13 Gift of the
Regents of the Smithsonian Institution/The Thomas Jefferson
Memorial Foundation and the Enid and Crosby Kemper
Foundation owned Jointly with Monticello/National Portrait
Gallery, Smithsonian Institution/Art Resource, NY; pp. 16,
22, 29b North Wind Picture Archives; p. 19 Museum of the
City of New York/Corbis; pp. 20, 21 Craig Brewer/Photodisc
Green/Getty Images; p. 27 Rick Bowmer/AP Wide World
Photos; p. 30 Steve Starr/Corbis; p. 33 Ron Chapple/
Taxi/Getty Images; p. 37 Stapleton Collection/ Corbis;
p. 39 Harry S. Truman Library; p. 45 Photo DC.

Every effort has been made to contact copyright holders
of any material reproduced in this book. Any omissions
will be rectified in subsequent printings if notice is given
to the publisher.

Some words are shown in bold, **like
this.** You can find out what they
mean by looking in the glossary.

Contents

Recording Important Events

Throughout history, people have created documents so they will have a record of an important event. Documents may tell stories about how people lived, how significant discoveries were made, or what occurred during a war.

Documents that provide a historical record of something can be divided into two categories: **primary sources** and **secondary sources.**

Primary sources

When historians are studying what happened in the past, they prefer to use primary sources. This term refers to documents that provide a firsthand account of an event. Primary sources can include letters, diaries, newspaper articles, **pamphlets,** and other papers that were written by people who witnessed or were directly involved in an event.

Primary sources can also include official papers that were carefully planned, often with much discussion and argument. The people involved in the planning and writing of these papers were careful to make sure the words in the documents expressed the exact thoughts and ideas they wanted them to. Official papers are usually a clear record of just what the authors intended to say.

On September 25, 1789, **Congress** proposed twelve **amendments** to the **Constitution**. Ten of these amendments were **ratified** and became the first ten amendments of the Constitution, or the Bill of Rights.

Members of the First Continental Congress **debated** almost every suggestion proposed at the meeting.

Primary sources tell us, in the words of the people who lived during that time, what really happened. They are a kind of direct communication that has not been filtered through a lot of sources. Often, stories that are passed verbally from person to person change as they are told and retold. Facts may become muddled and confused, and information may be added or left out. Soon, the original story has completely changed.

This is why primary sources are so important. Over time, facts can be changed or twisted, either accidentally or on purpose, so unwritten accounts of what happened in the past can be incorrect. To find out what really happened and why, historians rely on printed or handwritten primary sources.

Secondary sources

Secondary sources are accounts of events written by people who have studied primary sources. They read letters, journals, and other firsthand accounts, and then write their own version based on their research.

Storing Valuable Documents

Because **primary source** documents provide an important record of historical events, they are considered valuable. For that reason, the paper-and-ink documents are carefully handled and stored so that they will last a long time.

Documents that are considered valuable records of United States history are kept in several different places. The two institutions that hold most of these historical records are the Library of Congress and the National Archives and Records Administration, or NARA.

The Library of Congress

The Library of Congress is in Washington, D.C. It is a **federal** institution and also the largest library in the world. The library holds about 120 million items, including maps, books, and photographs. Its collection is available to members of **Congress** as well as the rest of the American public.

The NARA

The NARA is another government agency. It manages all federal records. Besides paper documents, the NARA also holds films, photographs, posters, sound and video recordings, and other types of government records. The original documents in the NARA collection provide a history of the U.S. government. They also tell

Tom Clark was the Attorney General of the United States from 1945–49. Here he looks at the Bill of Rights as it was displayed in the 40s.

Visitors wait in line at the NARA on July 4, 2001, to view the original copies of the **Declaration of Independence**, the **Constitution**, and the Bill of Rights.

the story of American settlement, industry, and farming. In fact, documents and other **artifacts** detailing almost every aspect of American history can be found in the NARA collection.

Most of the documents at the NARA are stored in specially designed boxes. Since paper is made from plants, it contains acids. Over time, these acids can discolor paper, turning it so dark that the ink on it cannot be read. For this reason, NARA storage boxes are acid-free. The boxes are stored in fireproof, locked **stacks** at the NARA's 41 different facilities. The temperature and **humidity** in NARA storage areas are carefully controlled, because heat and humidity can **deteriorate** documents.

What Is the Bill of Rights?

The Bill of Rights is a part of the United States **Constitution.** It lists the rights of every American and is made up of ten **amendments.**

The Constitutional Convention

The idea of a Bill of Rights started in the late 1700s. At that time, U.S. political leaders were trying to decide what kind of government would be best for the new nation. In May 1787, **delegates** met at a gathering called the Constitutional Convention to discuss improving the nation's government. Since 1781, the country had been operating under guidelines set up by the **Articles of Confederation.** The United States was becoming weak under the Articles, and the leaders agreed that they needed to be reviewed and changed. Shortly after opening the meeting, the delegates agreed that instead of making changes to the Articles of Confederation, they would start over and create a new model for government. The delegates decided to write a constitution.

After much **debate** and corrections, the Articles of Confederation were **adopted** by **Congress** on November 15, 1777.

A bill of rights rejected

As delegates came up with ideas and wording for the Constitution, some said they would like to include a list of rights guaranteed to each **citizen**—or a bill of rights. By that time, most state constitutions included a bill of rights to make sure certain rights were recognized by the government. Delegates who were **anti-federalist**

felt that adding a bill of rights to the Constitution would be a promise to citizens that they had nothing to fear from the government.

Most delegates wanted to concentrate on writing the Constitution. They did not believe that a bill of rights was important. Since the majority of delegates felt this way, the Bill of Rights was not written until 1789.

Today, the Bill of Rights is on display at the NARA in Washington, D.C., along with the **Declaration of Independence** and the Constitution. Together, these three documents make up what are called the **Charters** of Freedom.

The Virginia Declaration of Rights

One of the examples for the U.S. Bill of Rights was the Virginia Declaration of Rights. This document became official in Virginia on June 12, 1776. Thomas Jefferson used some of its ideas in the opening paragraphs of the Declaration of Independence. The Virginia Declaration of Rights was written by George Mason, a wealthy Virginia planter. Mason was a delegate to the Constitutional Convention in 1787. He was also one of three men who refused to sign the Constitution because it did not have a bill of rights.

One difference between the Virginia Declaration of Rights and the U.S. Bill of Rights has to do with religion. While the Bill of Rights states that Americans should be tolerant of all religions, Mason's Declaration of Rights says freedom of religion is a right, not just something to be tolerated.

George Mason

Why a Bill of Rights?

The government outlined by the **Constitution** had more powers than the old **confederation** government. Among those powers was the ability to tax U.S. **citizens,** to make laws regarding elections, and to organize an army. Some Americans felt that a strong government could use those powers to take away some of their rights. For this reason, they thought the Constitution should include a list of rights that the government could not take away from the people.

British oppression

Many Americans remembered what life was like before the **colonies** declared independence from Great Britain. They remembered how British **Parliament** made them pay taxes, but did not give them a voice

The Boston Tea Party was a result of unfair taxes imposed on the **colonists.** To fight the British tea tax, colonists dressed as Indians, boarded ships, and dumped all the tea into Boston Harbor. Below, fellow colonists cheer during the event.

in government. They also recalled that the British had sent soldiers into the colonies to stand guard and make sure the people did not rebel. The last thing Americans wanted was another government that would force its power on them the way the British government did. This was another reason why they wanted a list of rights in the Constitution.

James Madison—who was later responsible for pushing the **amendments** through **Congress** that became the Bill of Rights— was against the idea of a bill of rights at first. Like many other **federalists,** Madison believed that the Constitution did not need a bill of rights. He believed the Constitution *was* a bill of rights.

Madison began to change his mind after he realized that some Americans did not support the Constitution because it had no bill of rights. With the help of his friend Thomas Jefferson, he began to understand why some Americans were worried. Citizens felt that a government run by the people, where the vote of the majority ruled, could affect a minority. In other words, those in the minority were concerned that their wishes would not count, and that they would be overrun by the majority.

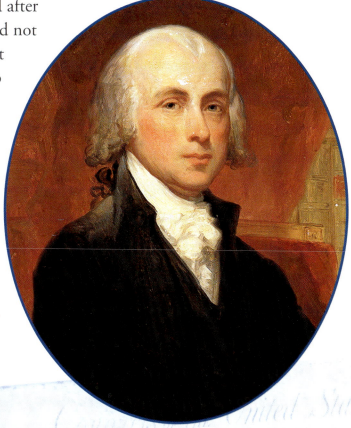

James Madison was very involved in planning what would appear in the Constitution and the Bill of Rights. In 1809, Madison became the fourth president of the United States.

The Constitution is Ratified

When the **delegates** to the Constitutional Convention were finished writing the **Constitution,** the document went to **ratifying** conventions in each state. At these meetings, delegates reviewed the document. Some states, such as Massachusetts, agreed to ratify the Constitution only after being told that members of the **House of Representatives** would soon start working on a bill of rights.

Members of state ratifying conventions—anticipating the addition of a bill of rights—drew up lists of **amendments** they wished to see added to the Constitution or included in a bill of rights. The nine states that ratified the Constitution presented 210 amendments to **Congress.** Some amendments were repeat requests, but 100 of them were completely original.

The new government

In June 1788, the Constitution was ratified. The new government under the Constitution began to operate in March 1789. The House of Representatives and the **Senate**—which together made up

In 1783, the United States nearly doubled with the addition of land to the west of the original thirteen colonies.

Know It

In his reelection **campaign** for representative, Virginia delegate James Madison—who had a large part in creating the Constitution—made a promise. He said that if the Constitution was ratified, he would push Congress to pass a bill of rights. Because of his promise, states that were unsure about ratifying the Constitution decided to do so.

Jefferson and the Bill of Rights

Thomas Jefferson, who was the president of the United States from 1801 to 1809, was an **ambassador** in Paris when the Constitution was **drafted**. After he read a copy of the finished Constitution, Jefferson wrote to his friend James Madison that he liked many things about it. But he did not like the fact that there was no bill of rights in the Constitution. Jefferson wrote that ". . . a bill of rights is what the people are entitled to against every government on earth, general or particular, and what no just government should refuse. . . ." Jefferson wrote similar letters to others in the United States as well. Many historians believe that Jefferson's encouragement provided the support Madison needed when he introduced the idea of a bill of rights to Congress.

what is often called the First Congress—opened their sessions in New York City that month. In April, George Washington was **inaugurated** as the first president of the United States.

The meetings of the House of Representatives during the first year were eventful. Congressmen were busy working on organizing the new government, and few seemed to care about working on a bill of rights.

Thomas Jefferson

Madison, however, remembered his campaign promise and kept it. He tried to get the House to set aside some time to discuss a bill of rights. Madison knew that many Americans disliked the amount of power given to Congress by the Constitution, and that adding a bill of rights might ease their worries. He also knew that **anti-federalists** wanted to change the Constitution and were planning to call a meeting very soon to do so.

Madison Presents His Ideas

On May 4, 1789, James Madison stood up in the **House of Representatives** to announce that he wanted to discuss the matter of a bill of rights before the end of the month. However, it was not until June 8 that he was able to present his ideas for a bill of rights. Madison made a long speech on that day. In it, he presented his ideas for **amendments** to the **Constitution.** Then he asked the House to discuss his ideas.

Many Congressmen complained when Madison suggested the discussion. They claimed that they were too busy with other, more important business to spend time on a bill of rights. Some said they should wait a while and give the Constitution a chance before they started changing it. Others thought that the Constitution covered all of the rights Madison mentioned in his speech, and that a bill of rights was unnecessary.

Anti-federalists want changes

Madison pushed for action. He said that many Americans were not happy with the Constitution. Some people, led by the **anti-federalists,** even wanted to rewrite it. The Congressmen knew this—in fact, several of them were the anti-federalist leaders who were unhappy with the present Constitution. These leaders had already drawn up a list of things they wanted to change about the Constitution.

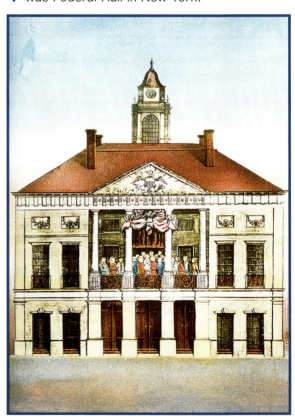

The first Capitol of the United States was Federal Hall in New York.

The House of Representatives said it would begin to consider a bill of rights soon, but did not name a specific date. It then went on with other business.

On June 12, the speech Madison made on June 8 was printed in a New York newspaper called the *Daily Advertiser.* The next day, the speech was printed in the *Gazette of the United States.* The public soon knew all about Madison's ideas for a bill of rights, and many people voiced their support.

DAILY ADVERTISER.
NEW-YORK, JUNE 12, 1789.
Congressional Intelligence.
HOUSE OF REPRESENTATIVES.

A Correspondent has favored us with the following copy of the Resolution proposed by the Hon. Mr. MADISON, in the House of Representatives, on Monday last, when the subject of AMENDMENTS was under consideration:—

Resolved, That the following amendments ought to be proposed by Congress to the legislatures of the states, to become, if ratified by three fourths thereof, part of the constitution of the United States.

First. That there be prefixed to the constitution a declaration—That all power is originally vested in, and consequently derived from the people.

That government is instituted, and ought to be exercised for the benefit of the people ; which consists in the enjoyment of life and liberty, with the right of acquiring and using property, and generally of pursuing and obtaining happiness and safety.

That the people have an indubitable, unalienable, and indefeasible right to reform or change their government, whenever it be found adverse or inadequate to the purposes of its institution.

Secondly. That in article 1st, section 2, clause 3, these words be struck out, to wit, "The number of representatives shall not exceed one for every thirty thousand, but each state shall have at least one representative, and until such enumeration shall be made." And that in place thereof be inserted these words, to wit, "After the first actual enumeration there shall be one representative for every thirty thousand, until the number shall amount to ____ after which the proportion shall be foregulated by Congress, that the number shall never be less than ____ nor more than ____ but each state shall after the first enumeration, have at least two representatives ; and prior thereto"

Thirdly. That in article 1st, section 6, clause 1, there be added to the end of the first sentence, these words, to wit:— "But no law varying the compensation last ascertained shall operate before the next ensuing election of representatives."

Excessive bail shall not be required in their persons, their papers, and their other ____ from all unreasonable searches, zures, shall not be violated by warrant issued without probable cause ported by oath or affirmation, particularly describing the place be searched, or the persons or to be seized.

In all criminal prosecutions, the accused shall enjoy the right to a ____ and public trial, to be informed the cause and nature of the accusation to be confronted with his accusers and the witnesses against him have a compulsory process for taining witnesses in his favor ; to have the assistance of counsel his defence.

The exceptions here or elsewhere in the constitution, made in favor of particular rights, shall not be so construed as to diminish the just importance of other rights retained by the people ; or as to enlarge the powers delegated by the constitution ; but either as actual limitations of such powers, or as inserted merely for greater caution.

Fifthly. That in article 1st, section 10, between clauses 1 and 2, be inserted this clause, to wit :
No state shall violate the equal rights of conscience, or the freedom of the press, or the trial by jury in criminal cases.

Sixthly. That article 3d, section 2, be annexed to the end of clause 2d, these words, to wit : but no appeal to such court shall be allowed where the value in controversy shall not amount to ____ dollars : nor shall any fact triable by jury, according to the course of common law, be otherwise re-examinable than may consist with the principles of common law.

Seventhly. That in article 3d, section 2, the third clause be struck out, and in its place be inserted the clauses following, to wit:
The trial of all crimes (except in cases of impeachments, and cases arising in the land or naval forces, or the militia when on actual service in time of war, or public danger,) shall be by an impartial jury of freeholders of the vicinage, with the requisite of unanimity for conviction, of the right of challenge, and other accustomed ____

How amendments are added to the Constitution

The men who **drafted** the Constitution knew the best kind of government was one that allowed for change. Because of this, they included a procedure in the Constitution that provided for amendments, or changes, to the document. Changes can be done in two ways. The first way is for two-thirds of the members of both the House of Representatives and the **Senate** to agree that the amendment is necessary. The second way is for states to send **delegates** to a constitutional convention, where two-thirds of them must agree to propose the amendment. So far, the second way has never been used. Amendments are placed at the end of the Constitution. The only way an amendment can be **repealed,** or removed, is with another amendment.

The House Works on the Bill of Rights

The **House of Representatives** put the matter of a bill of rights aside and continued to work on other business. On June 21, 1789, James Madison brought up the subject again. Congress **debated** about how to best go about considering a bill of rights. Finally, they set up a Committee of Eleven, made up of one representative from each state. There were only eleven states represented in **Congress** at that time, because Rhode Island and North Carolina had not yet **ratified** the **Constitution.**

The members of the Committee of Eleven were told to go over all the **amendments** they had. These amendments included Madison's, as well as those from the state ratifying conventions. On July 28, the committee reported back to the House. They had kept nearly all

The Committee of Eleven

The members of the Committee of Eleven were:

Delegate	State
John Vining, chairman	Delaware
Abraham Baldwin	Georgia
Egbert Benson	New York
Elias Boudinot	New Jersey
Aedanus Burke	South Carolina
George Clymer	Pennsylvania
George Gale	Maryland
Nicholas Gilman	New Hampshire
Benjamin Goodhue	Massachusetts
James Madison	Virginia
Roger Sherman	Connecticut

George Clymer

Abraham Baldwin

of Madison's amendments and kept only a few of the states' amendments.

The committee of the whole

On August 13, Congress began debating the amendments presented by the Committee of Eleven. The **delegates** went into a committee of the whole. This meant that they did not have to follow strict **parliamentary procedure** and could share opinions and information informally. When they wanted a formal discussion or a formal vote, they ended the committee of the whole and went back to being the House of Representatives, following parliamentary procedure.

On August 18, 1789, the committee of the whole declared its work complete. They then began considering the amendments as the House of Representatives. Since they had already considered the amendments as a committee, the delegates did not spend a lot of time discussing them. The House voted to put the amendments separately at the end of the Constitution.

This photograph shows the first page of the original Bill of Rights, as it appeared after it was presented to and approved by the U.S. **Senate** in 1789.

James Madison had hoped to weave the amendments into the Constitution, instead of tacking them on at the end. But many delegates disagreed. The men at the Constitutional Convention, they said, had put their names to what they felt was a complete document. Even President Washington had signed his name to the Constitution, as had Madison himself. Rewriting the words these men had signed their names to would dishonor their hard work, and make it seem as though they had made mistakes.

The Senate Takes Over

On August 22, 1789, after several weeks of discussion and planning, the **House of Representatives** named a committee to rewrite the revised **amendments** and put them in order. The committee presented its final report of the amendments on August 24. They had a total of seventeen amendments.

The Senate at work

Congress had copies of the final report printed by Thomas Greenleaf, a printer in New York City. Then the copies were delivered to the **Senate** for review. Some of the senators felt that working on the amendments was taking time away from more important business. Still, for two weeks the Senate worked on the seventeen amendments. They rewrote some of the amendments and combined others. When the senators were finished with their version of the amendments, there were twelve instead of seventeen. The twelve amendments were then sent back to the House, where they were reviewed again.

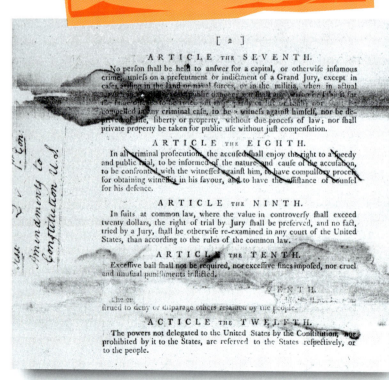

Know It

A printed version of the seventeen articles approved by the House and sent to the Senate is in the NARA. That is why we know how the amendments changed as they were **debated** in Congress. On this document are notes in ink. A few other such documents with notations are also in the NARA collection.

Here is the second page of the original Bill of Rights that was presented to and passed by the U.S. Senate.

An expensive piece of paper

The House most likely had Thomas Greenleaf print 100 copies of the seventeen amendments sent to the Senate on August 24. Five copies are known to exist today. Collectors pay large sums of money for copies of the amendments when they go up for sale. For example, in October 2002, a Greenleaf copy of the seventeen amendments was sold at an auction in New York City for $288,500!

The committee of six

In the House, a committee of six **delegates** was named to discuss the Senate's changes. Three representatives, including Madison, and three senators were on the committee. The committee focused on the Senate changes that the House members disagreed with. When the committee submitted its report, the House considered the amendments to be in their final form. The committee also had copies printed by Thomas Greenleaf. Today, only two copies of this version of the Bill of Rights are known to exist.

On to the states

On September 25, 1789, Congress approved the final version of the twelve amendments and sent them to President Washington. On October 2, copies of the amendments were delivered to the state **legislatures.** Along with the copies was a letter written by the president asking the legislatures to **ratify** the amendments.

George Washington

Engrossing the Bill of Rights

After **Congress** approved the twelve **amendments** on September 25, 1789, it ordered them to be **engrossed.** William Lambert, a Congressional clerk, engrossed the Bill of Rights.

Parchment

When a document is engrossed, it is written with ink using a fancy form of writing, called calligraphy. The material on which it was written was parchment. Parchment is usually made from the skin of a sheep, calf, or goat. All fur or hair is stripped or scraped from the skin. Then it is stretched on a frame and scraped some more. As the skin dries, it becomes strong, like a thin piece of leather. Parchment was expensive in the 1700s and was made to last a long time. So, when a document was sent to be engrossed, it meant that those in charge of the document considered it to be final.

The engrosser's tools

Lambert used a pen called a quill to engross the Bill of Rights. Quills were made from duck, goose, swan, or pheasant feathers. Each quill was cut to a point and dipped into an inkwell. Some of the ink rose into the hollow quill, so the writer could write several words

Know It

In 1789, each of the then fourteen states was sent a copy of the Bill of Rights engrossed on parchment.

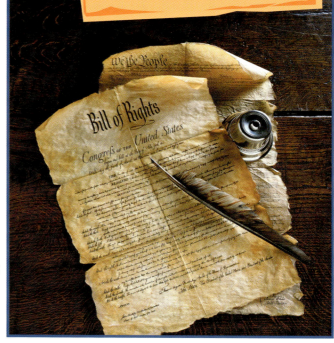

William Lambert used tools like these to engross the Bill of Rights in 1789.

before dipping it into the ink again. The ink used to engross the Bill of Rights was iron-gall ink, made from oak trees and several kinds of dye. While Lambert wrote, he spread a light coat of finely powdered **pumice** over the surface of the parchment. The pumice powder was used to keep the ink from spreading, or feathering.

Signing the parchment

Four people signed the Bill of Rights parchment: Speaker of the House Frances Muhlenberg, President of the **Senate** John Adams, Secretary of the Senate Samuel Otis, and Clerk of the House John Beckley. Because the parchment was signed in 1789, before the **amendments** went to the states for **ratification,** it contains the original twelve amendments. The first two amendments were not ratified, so they are not actually part of the Bill of Rights.

Virginia became the last state to ratify the amendments on December 15, 1791. At that time, Secretary of State Thomas Jefferson had 135 copies printed. By then, Congress had left New York City and was meeting in Philadelphia, Pennsylvania. So, Jefferson gave the job to Philadelphia printers Childs and Swaine.

Each of the fourteen 1789 engrossed copies of the Bill of Rights were signed by the same four people, because they thought this to be the final version.

The Ratification Process

Few records exist of the discussion and **debate** that occurred in state **legislatures** about the twelve **amendments**. Historians believe this lack of records is because by that time, most people did not feel that the amendments were important. They were concentrating on building homes and businesses in their newly independent country instead.

Two amendments not ratified

The first two amendments seem to have been the ones argued over most because they were not **ratified.** The first amendment said that there would be one representative in the House for every 30,000 people. It went on to explain the details of how this would work and ended by saying that there would be no less than 200 representatives in **Congress.** Disagreements over

A parade honoring Alexander Hamilton and the U.S. **Constitution** was held on Wall Street in New York City.

how U.S. **citizens** would be represented in Congress had been going on since the creation of the Constitution in 1787. The second amendment said that congressmen could not get pay raises between elections.

Ratification

To become official, the amendments had to be ratified by two-thirds of the states. Ratification continued until 1791. In February of that year Vermont officially became a state, making fourteen states altogether. This meant that eleven states had to ratify the amendments for them to become official.

Amendments three through twelve were ratified on December 15, 1791, when Virginia became the eleventh state to approve those ten amendments. Together, they make up the Bill of Rights. Today, December 15 is called Bill of Rights Day.

No law varying the compensation [payment] *for the services of the senators and representatives shall take effect, until an election of representatives shall have intervened* [happened].

Two hundred years to be ratified

The last amendment (so far) to the U.S. Constitution, Amendment 27, was added on May 7, 1992. This amendment was actually the second of the original twelve amendments to the Constitution included in the Bill of Rights sent to the states on September 25, 1789. The amendment states that Congress cannot give itself pay raises until after an election.

The First Amendment

When considering individual **amendments** in the Bill of Rights, it is important to understand how they came about. The United States had just gained independence from Great Britain after a long war. The war began in part because Britain's **Parliament** would not allow the **colonies** to be a part of the government. As Parliament imposed laws and taxes on the colonies, Americans felt that they were losing more and more of their freedoms and rights. Many of the amendments in the Bill of Rights were **drafted** in reaction to Britain's laws.

Amendment I

When Thomas Jefferson wrote to James Madison about what should be included in a bill of rights, he stated that the amendments must include freedom of religion. Madison agreed with him, and his suggestion for such an amendment comes first in the Bill of Rights. The beginning of the First Amendment states:

> *Congress shall make no law respecting an establishment of religion, or **prohibiting** the free exercise thereof;*

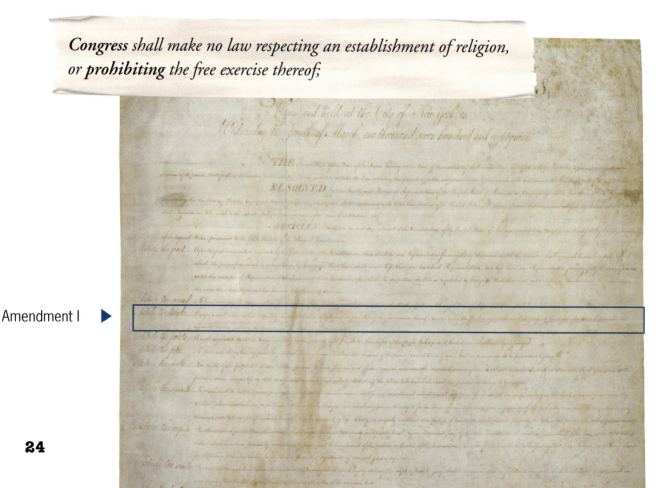

Amendment I ▶

Many of the Pilgrims who sailed to North America on the *Mayflower* were escaping Europe in order to practice their own religion.

Many of the first American settlers came to the colonies because they wanted to worship freely, in their own way. In Great Britain, there was an established church—a church that was approved by the government and received government money. Not everyone in Britain wanted to belong to this church, however, and sometimes people were **persecuted** for believing in another religion. Congress wanted to make sure that in the United States, people were free to worship as they pleased.

Members of Congress **debated** for a long time about just how to word this amendment. They finally agreed on the above wording, which states that Congress cannot make any laws that prevent Americans from practicing any religion. In addition, Congress cannot make any law that declares that one religion is better than another.

The First **Amendment** refers to freedom of religion when it states that "**Congress** shall make no law respecting an establishment of religion, or prohibiting the free exercise thereof." Religion is not the only part of this amendment. The First Amendment goes on to state, "or abridging [taking away] the freedom of speech, or of the press; or the right of the people peaceably to assemble, and to **petition** the Government for a redress [setting right] of grievances [complaints or sufferings]."

Besides stressing the importance of the freedom of religion, Jefferson wrote to Madison that the freedoms of speech and of the press were important. Madison and the rest of Congress agreed. In fact, Congress did not spend much time **debating** this part of the First Amendment. Everyone agreed that freedom of speech and of the press had to be included.

The next section of this amendment promises that Congress cannot make any laws that take away a person's right to speak freely on any issue. In addition, Congress can make no laws that prevent the press—that is, publications such as newspapers and magazines, as well as what appears on radio and television—from freedom of speech.

The First Amendment allows the press to publish its views without being punished.

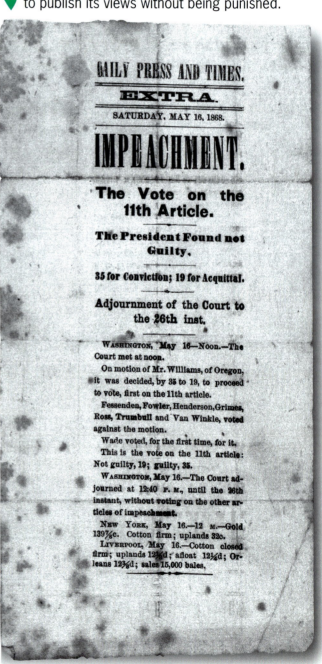

DAILY PRESS AND TIMES.
EXTRA.
SATURDAY, MAY 16, 1868.

IMPEACHMENT.

The Vote on the 11th Article.

The President Found not Guilty.

35 for Conviction; 19 for Acquittal.

Adjournment of the Court to the 26th inst.

WASHINGTON, May 16—Noon.—The Court met at noon.
On motion of Mr. Williams, of Oregon, it was decided, by 35 to 19, to proceed to vote, first on the 11th article.
Fessenden, Fowler, Henderson, Grimes, Ross, Trumbull and Van Winkle, voted against the motion.
Wade voted, for the first time, for it.
This is the vote on the 11th article: Not guilty, 19; guilty, 35.
WASHINGTON, May 16.—The Court adjourned at 12:40 P. M., until the 26th instant, without voting on the other articles of impeachment.
NEW YORK, May 16.—12 M.—Gold 139⅝c. Cotton firm; uplands 32c.
LIVERPOOL, May 16.—Cotton closed firm; uplands 12½d; afloat 12½d; Orleans 12⅝d; sales 15,000 bales.

When the United States declared war on Iraq in 2003, many people disagreed with the idea. All over the country, people protested the war. As long as the protest was peaceful, people were protected under the First Amendment.

Peaceable assembly

Another right named in this amendment is the freedom to assemble peaceably. This means that people can gather for any reason, including to protest something the government has done. As long as the gathering is a peaceful one, the government cannot get involved. However, if violence occurs, such as a **riot,** the government can stop it.

The section about "redress of grievances" means that Americans can speak out against their government without fear of being punished. However this must also be done peaceably.

Amendments II and III

The Second **Amendment** refers to the right of Americans to bear arms, or to own and carry guns. It states:

> *A well regulated **Militia**, being necessary to the security of a free State, the right of the people to keep and bear arms* [guns], *shall not be infringed* [taken away].

When this amendment was written, there were militias throughout the states. Militias were made up of **citizens** who used their own guns to defend their communities or states. The phrase "free states" shows that the states were concerned with keeping their individuality and their rights. In the late 1700s, most Americans believed that local militias offered the best protection. Because of that, they wanted their militias to be able to own and carry guns.

The next part of the amendment, "the right of the people to keep and bear arms," has been argued over for many years. Some people believe that **Congress** meant that only an army or a militia could own guns.

Colonists chase British soldiers across a bridge during the Battle of Concord, one of the first battles of the **Revolutionary War.**

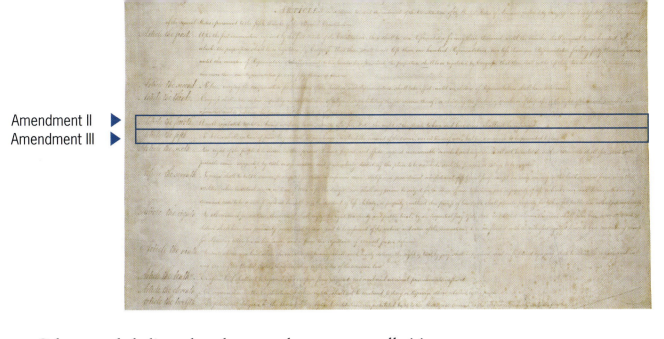

Amendment II ▶

Amendment III ▶

Other people believe that the amendment means all citizens can own guns. The wording of the amendment is unclear to many because of the commas and because at first it refers to a militia, but later says "the people." Most law experts agree that the founders meant that the people, or all citizens, have the right to keep and bear arms, or guns.

Amendment III

The Third Amendment is probably the one that has been used the least over the years. It states: "No Soldiers shall, in time of peace be quartered [housed] in any house, without the consent [permission] of the Owner, nor in time of war, but in a manner to be prescribed [directed] by law." The origin of this amendment can be traced to immediately before and during the Revolutionary War. Americans, especially in Massachusetts, were forced to allow British soldiers to stay in their homes. This practice angered many people. Congress wanted to make sure that no soldiers, including American soldiers, would be able to force their ways into American homes again.

Amendments IV and V

The Fourth **Amendment** says that:

> *The right of the people to be secure in the persons, houses, papers, and effects, against unreasonable searches and seizures* [take possession of], *shall not be violated* [broken], *and no Warrants* [papers authorizing search or arrest] *shall issue, but upon probable cause, supported by* **Oath** *or affirmation* [agreeing to], *and particularly describing the place to be searched, and the persons or things to be seized.*

The amendment states that law enforcement or government officials cannot force their way into someone's home to search for something unless there is "probable cause." That means that law enforcement officers must provide proof that they have good reasons for doing the search. If they want to enter someone's home, they must first ask permission. If they do not get permission, they must have "oath or affirmation." This usually means officers must get permission from a high authority, such as a judge, to do the search.

In many cases, dogs are used to aid police officers in the search for illegal drugs.

Amendment V

The Fifth Amendment states:

*No person shall be held to answer for a **capital**, or otherwise infamous crime, unless on a presentment* [notice] *or **indictment** of a **Grand Jury**, except in cases arising in the land or naval forces, or in the **Militia**, when in actual service in time of War or public danger; nor shall any person be subject for the same offence to be twice put in jeopardy* [risk of losing] *of life or limb; nor shall be compelled* [forced] *in any criminal case to be a witness against himself, nor be deprived* [have taken away] *of life, liberty, or property, without due process of law; nor shall private property be taken for public use, without just compensation* [payment].

First, this amendment says that a grand jury must indict persons for capital crimes, such as murder or kidnapping. The exception is when the person accused is in the armed forces during war or other emergencies. Then the amendment says that a person cannot be tried twice for the same crime. Next, a person cannot be a witness against himself—for example, a person does not have to testify at his or her own trial. It goes on to say that proper procedure must be followed, according to law, before a person is punished for a crime. Also, if a person's property is taken away for public use—for example, if someone property is needed to build a highway—that person must be paid fairly for the land.

There was little argument or discussion about the Fifth Amendment in the state **ratifying** conventions. The wording that Madison used when he first introduced this amendment in his speech on June 8, 1789, was barely changed in the final version.

Amendments VI and VII

The next two **amendments** in the Bill of Rights are about law. They state the rights that people accused of committing crimes have during the process they must go through to prove their guilt or innocence.

Amendment VI

The Sixth Amendment discusses how the people of the United States deal with people charged with crimes. It states:

> *In all criminal prosecutions* [accusations of wrongdoing], *the accused shall enjoy the right to a speedy and public trial, by an impartial* [fair] *jury of the State and district wherein the crime shall have been committed; which district shall have been previously ascertained* [determined] *by law, and to be informed of the nature and cause of the accusation; to be confronted* [faced] *with the witnesses against him; to have compulsory* [required] *process for obtaining witnesses in his favor, and to have the Assistance of Counsel for his defence.*

Basically, this amendment means that a person who is arrested and charged with committing a crime has the right to a speedy trial. At the trial, he or she will be judged by an impartial jury—that is, a jury that will act fairly. The trial will be in the district where the crime was

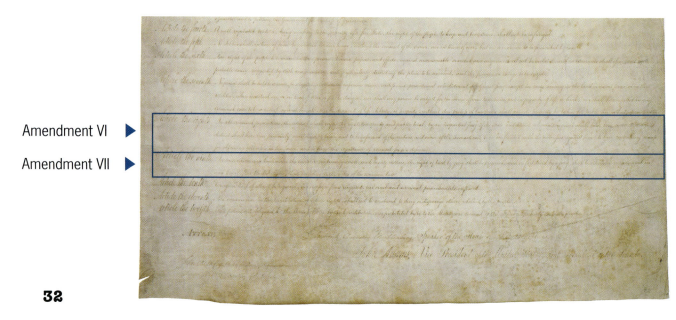

Amendment VI ▶

Amendment VII ▶

The Sixth Amendment guarantees that persons charged with a crime receive a speedy trial judged by a fair jury. The twelve-member jury here sits in the upper-right corner of the picture.

committed, and a person charged with a crime must know exactly what he or she is accused of doing. The accused, or the person charged with the crime, will be made aware of all those who will act as witnesses. The accused will be allowed to provide his or her own witnesses. "To have the Assistance of Counsel for his defence" means that the accused will always have the right to an attorney at a trial, even if he or she cannot afford to pay one.

Amendment VII

The Seventh Amendment says that:

In Suits at common law, where the value in controversy shall exceed twenty dollars, the right of trial by jury shall be preserved, and no fact tried by a jury shall be otherwise reexamined in any Court of the United States, than according to the rules of the common law.

This means that in lawsuits involving property worth more than twenty dollars—which was much more money in 1791 than it is today!—the person going to trial has the right to be tried by a jury. Then it says that once a case has been tried by a jury, it cannot go to trial again unless there is a law that states it can.

Amendments VIII, IX, and X

The Eighth and Ninth **Amendments** continue to discuss law and the process an accused person is promised.

Amendment VIII

The Eighth Amendment states that

> *Excessive **bail** shall not be required, nor excessive fines imposed, nor cruel and unusual punishments **inflicted**.*

If a person is arrested as a suspect in a crime, the bail required to allow that person to leave jail should not be extremely high. In addition, the fines or punishment for a crime should not be "cruel and unusual." This phrase has been used by people who are against the death penalty, because they believe that it is both cruel and unusual. It has also been used by those who wish to see better living conditions in prisons.

Know It

The bail **clause** in the Eighth Amendment is almost exactly the same as a clause from the English Bill of Rights Act of 1689. The Virginia Declaration of Rights also has this clause.

Amendment IX

The Ninth Amendment says that

> *The enumeration* [listing] *in the **Constitution** of certain rights shall not be construed* [understood] *to deny or disparage* [make less important] *others retained by the people*

When a bill of rights was being discussed by **Congress** in 1789, some Congressmen were concerned that listing rights in this way was dangerous. They could not list all of a person's rights, they argued.

With this amendment, they made sure that if rights the people considered to be theirs were not listed, they could still claim them as their rights.

Amendment X

The Tenth Amendment reads,

> *The powers not delegated to the United States by the Constitution, nor* **prohibited** *by it to the States, are reserved to the States respectively, or to the people.*

This amendment was included because **anti-federalists** worried about the **federal** government taking too many powers away from the states and the people.

Amendment VIII ▶
Amendment IX ▶
Amendment X ▶

Where Did These Rights Come From?

The United States **Constitution** gives certain powers to the three branches of government—executive, legislative, and judicial. But the Bill of Rights does not give the rights it names to the people of the U.S. Instead, those involved with creating the Bill of Rights were simply stating that they recognized that people have those rights. The rights existed before the Bill of Rights was written, and **Congress** was only acknowledging the rights and declaring that the government could not make laws against them.

Natural law

The privileges listed in the Bill of Rights were considered a part of what is called "natural law," or natural rights. The basic idea of natural law is that all human beings have certain rights. Often, those who spoke of these kinds of rights said that humans have "equal rights." The Bill of Rights names some of these rights. But while **drafting** the rights, members of Congress kept in mind that what they were including were the rights of *Americans*. In other words, Congress had a specific group of people in mind when defining these rights.

What about slaves?

At the time the Bill of Rights was written, there was a large group of people in the United States who had few rights. They were slaves. Slaves could not own land—and in those days to be allowed to vote, you had to own land.

Slave auctions were normal sights in most Southern states.

Slaves could not make wills or bear arms. Their homes and the things in them were not protected from seizure, because their bodies, homes, and possessions really belonged to their master. Slaves were rarely allowed trials by jury if they were accused of a crime. They were the property of their owners, not **citizens** with rights, so their owners could punish them as they wished.

Early U.S. government leaders knew that the Bill of Rights did not ensure rights to slaves. While the issue of slavery bothered many **delegates**—even some of those who owned slaves disagreed with the principle of slavery—they realized that the issue of slavery was too large and complicated to tackle at that time. The economy of the Southern states depended on slavery. If Congress tried to outlaw it, the fragile union of states would almost certainly have collapsed, because the states would be strongly divided over the issue.

One delegate's view

Charles Pinckney was a delegate to the Constitutional Convention from South Carolina, where many slaves lived. He said that some delegates did not want to discuss a bill of rights in the Constitutional Convention, or even later in Congress, because of slavery. In his words,

> *Such bills generally begin with declaring that all men are by nature born free. Now, we should make that declaration with a very bad grace, when a large part of our property consists in men who are actually born slaves.*

The Bill of Rights on Display

The parchment on which the Bill of Rights was **engrossed** was not put on public display until 1952. Before that, it was stored for a long time with other papers of the First **Congress.** At one time, it was even folded up many times, so now there are creases in the parchment. In the early 1900s, the parchment was stitched and glued along the top edge to a strip of fabric and put into a binder that contained the first acts of Congress.

Today, the parchment looks worn and old. The ink has faded, but the words can still be read.

On December 13, 1952, the Bill of Rights, along with the other **Charters** of Freedom, was moved from the Library of Congress to the NARA by a military escort.

President Truman addressed a crowd at the opening of the new display for the Charters of Freedom at the NARA on December 15, 1952.

Truman's speech

In 1952, President Harry Truman gave a speech at a ceremony on **Constitution Day**—September 17. The ceremony was held because the Constitution and the **Declaration of Independence** had just been put into special cases to **preserve** them. President Truman said in his speech that he hoped that one day the Bill of Rights parchment would be encased, too.

Not long after that, the Bill of Rights parchment was preserved and put into a special case. In December 1952, the Bill of Right went on display with the other Charters of Freedom at the NARA building in Washington, D.C.

Why the parchment lists twelve amendments

Catherine Nicholson is a senior **conservator** at the NARA in Washington, D.C. She states: "[a]n interesting fact is that the original record copy of the Bill of Rights in the National Archives actually lists the twelve proposed amendments. The two amendments not approved were listed as the first and second articles. What is today called the First Amendment was actually listed as the third article to be **ratified.** Bill of Rights Day is December 15, the day in 1791 when the required number of states had voted to ratify the amendments."

Restoring the Bill of Rights

In 1998, the public exhibit at the NARA closed so **conservators** could restore the documents. The Bill of Rights parchment was carefully removed from its case and closely checked for damage. Conservators used a binocular microscope to inspect the document, looking for any small flakes of ink that might be lifted up or breaking away from the paper. To restore flaking ink, conservators made a warm solution from gelatin and parchment scraps. The solution acted as a type of glue and was applied to flaking ink with a very fine tip sable brush. The conservator placed a tiny droplet of solution onto the lifting flake. The flake then relaxed and stuck to the surface of the parchment.

This conservator works to remove a document from its original protective encasement. Conservators must be extremely careful when working with old documents.

Applying humidity

After all of the flakes of ink were repaired, conservators applied **humidity** to the parchment. This helped make the parchment soft so that it could be flattened. The humidity helped remove creases that were created when it was folded. Once the parchment was flattened, it was put under tension and pressure to make sure it stayed flat while it dried.

The document was then put into a new case. The case is made from a strong substance called titanium and is filled with a gas called argon.

The exhibit reopens

In 2003, the new exhibit at the NARA **rotunda** in Washington, D.C., opened. The Bill of Rights, along with the other **Charters** of Freedom, are once again on display in the rotunda exhibit hall. The rotunda is on Constitution Avenue in downtown Washington, D.C.

See the Bill of Rights online

To see the Bill of Rights online, go to
http://www.archives.gov/exhibit_hall/charters_of_freedom/bill_of_rights/bill_of_rights.html.

The new exhibit at the NARA allows vistors to see all four pages of the **Constitution** (center), with the **Declaration of Independence** left of center, and the Rill of Rights right of center

A Conversation with a Conservator

Catherine Nicholson is Senior **Conservator** at the NARA.

How did you become interested in conservation work?

"When I was a high school student, devastating floods damaged many paintings, rare books, and drawings in Florence, Italy. The techniques devised to save these priceless treasures, based on knowledge of art history, artists' materials, and chemistry, fascinated me."

Ms. Nicholson was so interested in art that in college she earned a degree in art and art history. But once she graduated, she says, "I realized my strong interest in conservation and that I would need to study chemistry. I attended a graduate program in conservation of art and historic **artifacts** in which we learned about the ways in which a wide variety of materials **deteriorate,** about historic artists' methods and materials, and also learned to carry out conservation treatments based on that knowledge."

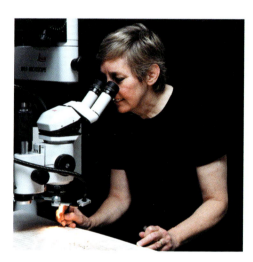

Catherine Nicholson uses a microscope to carefully restore a document.

What advice would you give young people interested in historic conservation?

Young people should "be curious about how things are made and what materials are used to make them. They should also enjoy problem solving and finding new solutions for problems.

The old Charters of Freedom display was under construction for several years, allowing conservators time to restore the old documents.

"In school, many different subjects are relevant," she continued. "A young person should be interested in [many related subjects or science]. So when you study chemistry, you should be interested in how chemical principles impact … the strength of paper or the **adhesion** of ink to paper, or the effect of light's energy on the colors of materials.

"Conservators have to look in many different books and sources to find information that is relevant to understanding their work. Enjoying making and understanding art and crafts is also very helpful. A conservator needs to do the very find handwork that takes good dexterity and a lot of patience."

What has been the highlight of your career?

Ms. Nicholson counts being one of the conservators selected to work on the **Charters** of Freedom as one of the highlights of her job. "I never dreamed when I started out that my career would bring me to this awe-inspiring and challenging responsibility. When we used a special tool to cut into the first sealed Charters encasement, we didn't know what the results might be. The encasement had been sealed almost 50 years ago and filled with helium gas. We didn't know if opening the sealed encasement and letting air in for the first time in 50 years would have an effect. We had done much research. But there is the moment in which all the **theoretical** study must be considered and careful action taken."

The Past Helps Us Understand the Present

Many Americans spoke of the need for a bill of rights when the **Constitution** was being **drafted.** However, by the time the Bill of Rights was **ratified** in 1791, most Americans paid little attention to it. Today, the Bill of Rights is considered one of the nation's most important documents, and its principles are tested daily.

When James Madison sponsored the Bill of Rights in 1789, he probably did not realize how far-reaching his words would be. He seemed to be able to predict what issues would be important not only to the eighteenth-century United States, but also far into the future. Many historians call Madison a genius.

Maintaining our national heritage

The **preservation** work done on the Bill of Rights and other documents at the NARA is important. Ms. Nicholson explained: "The National Archives holds the permanently valuable records of the United States government. These records help document the rights of **citizens,** the

Visitors look at the **Charters** of Freedom in the old NARA exhibit. The new exhibit allows visitors to view four pages of the Constitution, instead of just two as before.

actions of the **federal** government, and the national experience. Some records are personal and of great importance to a citizen or his or her relatives and descendants.

"But others," she continued, "are broad statements of our rights as citizens, the philosophy [beliefs] of our government's founders, and evidence [proof] of our national experience, the bad and the good, the tragic and the inspiring. These items make up our national **heritage** and help our citizens to remember our past, understand our present situation, and have bold dreams for the future that faces us and our descendants." For this reason, Ms. Nicholson explained, "It is important to preserve these records because they help us recall who we are as a nation and what we stand for and of the need to be **vigilant** in support of our rights."

Without the **Declaration of Independence,** the Constitution, and the Bill of Rights, the United States would not be the same nation. These documents improved our way of life and created the strong government that we have today.

Glossary

adhesion ability to stick, such as how glue sticks to paper

adopt accept and put into action

ambassador person from one country sent on a government mission to another country

amendment change; in the Constitution, amendments are formal changes voted on by states

anti-federalist member of a political group that was against a strong central, or federal, government

Articles of Confederation first governing document of the United States, in effect from 1776 until 1781

artifact something made by human skill or work, such as pottery, a weapon, or clothing

bail payment specified by a court to allow a person accused of a crime to leave jail until his or her trial

campaign organized operation with the goal of achieving a certain result; in politics, the result is an election

capital in crime, serious crime such as murder or kidnapping

charter official document granting, guaranteeing, or showing the limits of the rights and duties of the group to which it is given

citizen person who lives in a city or town and owes loyalty to a government and is protected by it

clause separate article in a formal document

colonist person who lives in a colony

colony settlement in a new territory that is tied to an established nation

confederation agreement of support between political bodies or people

Congress formal meeting of delegates for discussion and usually action on some question

conservator person who cares for, restores, and repairs items kept for historical or other reasons

constitution document that outlines the basic principles of a government

debate argument that follows certain rules of procedure

Declaration of Independence document in which the American colonies formally declared independence from Great Britain in 1776

delegate person sent as a representative to a meeting or conference

deterioration wear and tear, often due to exposure to heat, light, or moisture

draft sketchy or unfinished form of a piece of writing

engross prepare the final handwritten or printed text of an official document

excessive large amount

federal one central government that oversees smaller units; the smaller units, such as states, also have their own governments

federalist member of a political group that believed in having a strong, centralized government

grand jury jury that examines evidence to determine if a person should be accused of a crime

heritage something handed down from previous generations or gained through history

House of Representatives group of people that make laws for the United States humidity amount of moisture in the air

inaugurate to enter into office with a
ceremony

indictment statement that shows strong
disapproval

inflict put upon; imposed upon

legislature group of elected individuals who
make laws for those who elect them

militia citizens banded together in a
military unit

oath promise made in front of witnesses

pamphlet booklet with no cover, usually made
of paper folded into smaller parts

Parliament supreme lawmaking body in Great
Britain

parliamentary procedure specific way to hold
meetings, based on certain orderly rules
and systems

persecuted harassed or bothered

petition formal written request, often signed
by many people

preservation care and restoration of

primary source original copy of a journal,
letter, newspaper, document, or image

prohibit forbid; not allow

pumice powdery substance made of glass from
volcanoes

ratify vote to officially approve or accept

repeal officially remove or recall a decision
or law

Revolutionary War American fight for
independence from British rule between
1775–1783

riot public violence, disturbance, or disorder

rotunda round building, often covered with
a dome, or round room

secondary source written account of an event
by someone who studied a primary source
or sources

Senate upper and smaller branch of a legislature
in the United States

stack structure of bookshelves for storing
books, often used in libraries

theoretical arrived at using careful thought,
but not based on factual experience

vigilant careful and watchful

More Books to Read

Burgan, Michael. *The Bill of Rights*. Minneapolis: Compass Point Books, 2001.

Hossell, Karen Price. *The United States Constitution*. Chicago: Heinemann
Library, 2004.

Stein, R. Conrad. *The National Archives*. Danbury, Conn.: Franklin Watts, 2002.

Index